Food Plants

Learn about the many different kinds of plants we eat

ENCYCLOPÆDIA
Britannica®

CHICAGO LONDON NEW DELHI PARIS SEOUL SYDNEY TAIPEI TOKYO

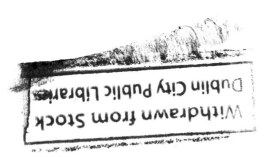

Food Plants

I N T R O D U C T I O N

Is the tomato a fruit or a vegetable? What crop was buried with the Egyptian pharaohs? When is a nut not a nut? What are tubers?

In *Food Plants,* you'll discover answers to these questions and many more. Through pictures, articles, and fun facts, you'll learn about the great diversity of plant life found around the world.

To help you on your journey, we've provided the following signposts in *Food Plants*:

■ **Subject Tabs**—The coloured box in the upper corner of each right-hand page will quickly tell you the article subject.

■ **Search Lights**—Try these mini-quizzes before and after you read the article and see how much - *and how quickly* - you can learn. You can even make this a game with a reading partner. (Answers are upside down at the bottom of one of the pages.)

■ **Did You Know?**—Check out these fun facts about the article subject. With these surprising 'factoids', you can entertain your friends, impress your teachers, and amaze your parents.

■ **Picture Captions**—Read the captions that go with the photos. They provide useful information about the article subject.

■ **Vocabulary**—New or difficult words are in **bold type**. You'll find them explained in the Glossary at the end of the book.

■ **Learn More!**—Follow these pointers to related articles in the book. These articles are listed in the Table of Contents and appear on the Subject Tabs.

Britannica
LEARNING LIBRARY

Have a great trip!

Groves of olive trees cover the hills near the city of Jaén in southern Spain.
© Michael Busselle/Corbis

Food Plants

TABLE OF CONTENTS

Britannica®
LEARNING LIBRARY

DID YOU KNOW?

The French term for 'potato' is *pomme de terre*, which means 'apple of the earth'. This may be because apples and potatoes have a similar texture (feel), size, and shape.

Fruit Tree Royalty

The apple tree is a hardy plant that is grown in more parts of the world than any other fruit tree. That's why the apple has often been called the 'king of fruits'.

Even though it is five-sixths water, the apple has vitamins, minerals, and **carbohydrates**. Before the science of nutrition told us how to eat

Colourful apple varieties.
© Royalty-Free/Corbis

healthily, people already knew that 'an apple a day keeps the doctor away'.

Apples are grown for eating, cooking, and making juice. 'Eating' apples are crisp and juicy, with a tangy smell. They may be red, green, greenish yellow, pink, or orange. 'Cooking' apples are firm. 'Juice' apples are used to make apple juice and cider. Apples are also preserved as jams, jellies, apple butter, and chutneys. And applesauce - made by stewing and, often, sweetening apples - is popular in many places.

If you plant the seeds of a good-tasting apple, you will probably be disappointed by the fruit that the new tree produces. Branches, as well as seeds, have to be used to produce the best apples. The process is called 'grafting'. Apple trees need well-drained soil to grow. They also need a period of cool winter weather to rest before the fruit-growing season.

There are many signs that humans discovered the apple a long time ago. There are pictures of apples carved on stone by **Stone Age** people. Apples are mentioned in the Bible. Although some kinds of apple grow wild in North America, the apples Americans eat come from varieties that were brought from Europe. John Chapman, an early American planter better known as Johnny Appleseed, helped to spread these varieties far and wide. Apple pie, in fact, is a symbol of America.

LEARN MORE! READ THESE ARTICLES…
BANANAS • GRAPES • MAPLE

SEARCH LIGHT

Why is the apple called the 'king of fruits'?

Apples must be handled carefully to avoid bruising. Here a worker gently picks apples ready for harvesting.
© Royalty-Free/Corbis

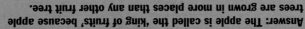

Answer: The apple is called the 'king of fruits' because apple trees are grown in more places than any other fruit tree.

7

SEARCH LIGHT

Plantains are
a) bananas that
   aren't sweet.
b) yellow bananas.
c) mushy brown
   bananas.

Fruit of Gold

A banana plant may grow to a height of 6 metres or more, but it is considered to be an **herb** rather than a tree. Instead of a trunk, it has a **stalk** made up of leaves rolled tightly around each other. From the stalk grows a big bunch of 50 to 200 individual bananas. Only one bunch grows on each plant. The bunch is made up of several clusters. Each cluster has 10 to 20 bananas. After harvesting, the plant is cut down. A new one then grows from an underground stem.

Farm worker on a banana plantation in Oman, in the Middle East.
© Christine Osborne/Corbis

Bananas grow only where it is warm and wet all the time, which is why people in cold countries may never see a banana plant. They love to eat the bananas, though. That's why banana farms called **plantations** are a big business in South Asia, Africa, Central and South America, and the islands of the Caribbean Sea. But Asia is where bananas originally came from.

Most everyone knows what happens to a banana that has sat around too long. It gets brown and mushy. So bananas have to be picked while they're still hard and bright green. They may have a long trip ahead of them - usually thousands of kilometres from the plantation to the grocery store. Refrigerated ships keep the bananas from ripening too soon, and then special heat and moisture treatments help them to ripen on schedule.

Bananas are used in making delicious cream pies, cakes, breads, and fruit salads. Many people's favourite banana dessert is the banana split ice-cream treat. But not all bananas are eaten as fruit. Some varieties never get sweet. These bananas, called 'plantains', are cooked and served as a vegetable.

LEARN MORE! READ THESE ARTICLES…
JACKFRUIT • MANGOES • PALM

DID YOU KNOW?

The largest banana split ever made was reported to be a little over seven kilometres long.

Bunches of bananas hang on a plant before being harvested and exported from the Caribbean island of Grenada in the West Indies.
© Dave G. Houser/Corbis

Answer: a) bananas that aren't sweet.

SEARCH LIGHT

Which of the following is not mentioned as a member of the cabbage family?
a) broccoli
b) cauliflower
c) carrot
d) Brussels sprouts

The 'Head' of a Vegetable Family

Cabbage has been grown for food since ancient times. Nearly 3,000 years ago, the Greek poet Homer mentioned it in his story-poem the *Iliad*.

Wild cabbage is native to the shores of the Mediterranean Sea. It also grows wild on the sea cliffs of Great Britain. The ancient Romans probably planted it there. Cabbages have thick moist leaves with a waxy coating. The leaves are often grey-green or blue-green in colour. Cabbage plants like cool weather and deep rich soil.

Two heads of cauliflower.
© Ed Young/Corbis

Over hundreds of years, many vegetables have been developed from the wild cabbage. Some are used for garden decoration or for feeding animals. But people eat many kinds. The cabbage group includes the common cabbage, cauliflower, broccoli, Brussels sprouts, and several other vegetables. They are rich in vitamins and minerals and low in **calories**.

The common, or head, cabbage has a tight bunch of leaves (the head) around a centre stem. People eat the leaves raw or cook them. Cabbage soup is a popular dish in much of eastern Europe. Finely chopped raw cabbage is the main ingredient in a salad called 'coleslaw'. If sliced-up cabbage is salted and put away for a long time, it goes through a chemical change. The result is sauerkraut, a popular dish in Germany. In Korea cabbage is a major ingredient in the traditional dish called *kimchi*.

Cauliflower has a head of tight thick white flowers. People eat the flowers either raw or cooked. Broccoli has bright green loosely clustered flowers. People eat these flowers along with the tender stalks. Brussels sprout plants have many little cabbage-like heads instead of one large head at the top.

LEARN MORE! READ THESE ARTICLES
GRAPES • PALM • TOMATOES

DID YOU KNOW?
In France a popular term for a loved one is *petit choux*, which means 'little cabbage'.

There are more than a hundred varieties of cabbage. Common (or head) cabbage is pictured here.
© Eric Crichton/Corbis

Answer: c) The carrot is not part of the cabbage family.

Fig trees grow only in hot dry climates. Shown here is the fruit of the fig tree as it ripens.
© Richard T. Nowitz/Corbis

Poor Man's Food

In Mediterranean countries the fig is used so widely, both fresh and dried, that it is called the 'poor man's food'. The soft juicy fruit of the fig tree cannot remain fresh for long in the hot **climate** where it grows. So it has to be dried in the sun before it is sent to the market. Fresh or dried, the fig is packed with food value.

Figs were first found growing around the Mediterranean Sea. It's no surprise then that figs still grow in the countries bordering the Mediterranean—including Turkey, Greece, Italy, and Spain. Spanish missionaries introduced the fig tree to Mexico and California. The entire fig crop in the United States comes from California.

There are four main types of figs: caprifig, Smyrna, White San Pedro, and Common. When a fig is introduced into another country, a new name is often given to it. The Smyrna fig became known as the Calimyrna fig in California.

Fig plants are either bushes or small trees. Fig trees are easily grown from **cuttings** off an adult tree. The fruit occurs either singly or in pairs. The trees produce two or three crops a year.

The best-tasting dried figs are those that have been allowed to dry partly on the tree. The figs are then laid out on trays to finish drying in the sun. Turning and moving them about while they dry improves their quality. Most dried figs are eaten in their natural form, though many are ground into a paste to be used in bakery products.

SEARCH LIGHT

Why would the fact that so many people eat figs earn it the nickname 'poor man's food'? (Hint: Food costs money.)

LEARN MORE! READ THESE ARTICLES…
GRAPES • NUTS • OLIVE

DID YOU KNOW?
There are more than 900 members of the fig group. One of them, the Bo tree, or pipal, is sacred in India. It is believed to be the tree under which the Buddha sat when he attained enlightenment.

Answer: Poor people can't afford many kinds of food but can always eat the figs found growing wild.

13

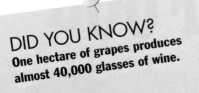

**This worker is collecting bunches of grapes
at harvest time. Green and red table grapes are
an excellent source of vitamin A.**
© Ted Streshinsky/Corbis

Fruit of the Vine

Grapes grow wild in wooded and warmer regions of the Northern **Hemisphere**. And people have raised grapes in these regions for thousands of years. Grapes have been taken to South Africa, South America, and Australia and grown with great success. There are about 60 different grape plants, as well as thousands of varieties.

The grape plant is a woody vine. A vine is a kind of plant that can't stand up by itself. It has stems called tendrils that cling to things and support the plant. An untrimmed vine may reach a length of 15 metres. Grapes are berries that grow in bunches on the vine. Grapes come in many colours - pale green, yellow, red, purple, or black. Some grapes have a white powdery coating.

The growing of grapes is called 'viticulture'. People don't usually grow grapes by planting seeds. Instead, they take cuttings off a vine that is already growing. These cuttings spend a year or so in **nurseries**, waiting to grow roots. When they have roots, they're ready to grow outside.

SEARCH LIGHT

The growing
of grapes
is called
a) 'vineculture'.
b) 'viticulture'.
c) 'grapiculture'.

Table grapes.
© Craig Lovell/Corbis

Another method of grape growing is called layering. In layering, the branch of a full-grown vine is bent into a curve and made to grow along the ground. New shoots and roots soon grow from this part of the branch. These are cut off from the parent vine and replanted as new vines.

Grapes are high in sugar. Different types are used for different purposes. Some are eaten fresh. Others are dried out to make raisins. But most are squeezed for their juice. Some grape juice is put through a process called 'fermentation' that changes some sugar into alcohol. The product that results is called 'wine'.

LEARN MORE! READ THESE ARTICLES…
APPLES • OLIVE • ORANGES

Answer: b) 'viticulture'.

SEARCH LIGHT

Most fruit grows on branches. Where does jackfruit grow?

The Largest Tree-Borne Fruit

The largest fruit that grows on trees is the jackfruit. And when we say it grows on trees, we mean it - the fruit grows on the main trunk of the tree and not on the branches. That's because it is so heavy that the branches can't support it - they would break right off!

A young Indonesian boy carrying jackfruits.
© Bennett Dean—Eye Ubiquitous/Corbis

So how big is this fruit? Well, a single jackfruit can weigh over 36 kilos! It sometimes reaches 90 centimetres long and almost 60 centimetres around. The jackfruit tree is also very large. It looks something like a large oak tree and grows to a height of 15 to 20 metres.

Jackfruit grows in the warm regions of Asia. It's grown widely in tropical countries where it is warm and rains a lot, such as the Philippines. There are many varieties of jackfruit. Some of the popular ones include Black Gold, Galaxy, and Honey Gold.

Like its cousin the mulberry, jackfruit is a compound fruit. This means that it has many, many seeds and that each seed surrounded by its **pulp** is a separate fruit. The big jackfruit you see is like a huge container holding all the little fruits together.

Young jackfruits are green. They turn brownish yellow when ripe. Raw jackfruit is cooked like a vegetable, though the sweet pulp surrounding the seeds can be eaten fresh. The seeds can be boiled or roasted and eaten like chestnuts.

Jackfruit has other uses too. The wood is a valuable hardwood like teak. It is used for making many things, especially furniture. Dried jackfruit leaves are used as fuel for cooking fires, while the green leaves provide **fodder** for goats.

DID YOU KNOW?
Ripe jackfruits have a strong odour before they're cut open. Some people compare the smell to that of rotting onions! But once you cut into the ripe fruit, it smells more like pineapples or bananas.

LEARN MORE! READ THESE ARTICLES...
BANANAS · ORANGES · PALM

Jackfruit is a distant cousin of the fig. It can grow to tremendous size.
© Liu Liqun/Corbis

Answer: Jackfruit grows on tree trunks. It's too heavy for branches.

17

SEARCH LIGHT

What colour are lemons when they are picked from the tree?

Sweet, but Oh So Sour!

The lemon is a **citrus** fruit, a family of fruits that includes limes, grapefruit, and oranges. Lemons grow on small trees and spreading bushes. The trees can grow quite tall if they are not trimmed. Their leaves are reddish when young, but they gradually turn green. Some lemon trees have sharp thorns next to the leaves.

Lemon flowers are large and may grow singly or in small clusters. The new buds of the lemon flower have a reddish tint. As they blossom, the inside of the flower turns white. Lemon flowers have a lovely sweet scent. This is one of the reasons that people like to have lemon trees in their gardens.

Lemon trees bloom throughout the year. The fruit is usually picked while it is still green. It can be damaged easily, so pickers wear gloves and have to be careful when handling the fruit. The fruit is stored for three or more months until its colour has changed to an even yellow.

The lemon fruit is oval and covered with a **rind** that is yellow when ripe. Inside, the flesh (or pulp) is divided into eight to ten segments that contain small pointed seeds. The pulp and its juice are rich in vitamin C. Lemon flavour is used in many foods, and many people put it in their tea. But the juice is very sour.

Some other important products provided by the lemon are lemon oil and pectin. In some places, the oil is used in perfumes and soaps. Pectin is what makes jelly so thick and sticky. It is also used in some medicines.

DID YOU KNOW?
The substance that makes lemons so sour is called citric acid. In addition to being so sour, it is a very harsh substance - in fact, it's said that there's enough citric acid in a lemon to dissolve a pearl!

LEARN MORE! READ THESE ARTICLES...
MANGOES • ORANGES • TEA

Beautiful and fragrant, lemon trees usually bloom throughout the year.
© Ray Juno/Corbis

Answer: Lemons are usually picked while they are still green. They turn yellow after they have aged for a while.

DID YOU KNOW?
Fruit bats help spread mangoes by carrying the fruit to another perch, where they eat the flesh and drop the seed. The seed plants itself in the ground, and soon a small mango tree pops up there.

The Regal Tropical Fruit

Sweet, tasty, and wonderfully sticky - that's a mango! So many people like this fruit that it is sometimes called 'the queen (or king) of **tropical** fruits'. And not only does it taste good - it's good for you because it's full of vitamins.

But mangoes didn't always taste so good. Thousands of years ago they were small fruits that tasted like pine needles! At that time they grew only in some parts of Asia, such as India and Myanmar. Today they're grown in most tropical countries. There are even mango farms in the southern United States.

Fresh mangoes.
© W. Wayne Lockwood, M.D./Corbis

Mangoes come in many shapes, sizes, and colours. They can be oval or round or long and slender. They can be red, yellow, or green. The smallest mangoes are no bigger than plums. The biggest are up to 25 centimetres long and can weigh as much as 2.3 kilos.

No matter what size they are, though, all mangoes have a lot of very juicy yellow or orange fruit underneath a thin skin. In the middle of the fruit is a single flat seed.

Mangoes grow on tall trees. Take five elephants and put them on top of each other, and that's how high mango trees can grow. The trees are evergreen, which means they keep their leaves all year.

You can eat mangoes raw. Just wash them, peel them, cut them, and eat them. Or you can eat mangoes mixed in milk, like a mango smoothie. Mangoes are also used to make sauces and chutneys. In India, during festivals, you'll find mango leaves strung together hanging outside the front doors of many houses. This is because mangoes are believed to bring luck.

LEARN MORE! READ THESE ARTICLES…
APPLES • JACKFRUIT • LEMONS

The mango is one of the most important and widely grown fruits of the tropical world. Mangoes are a rich source of vitamins A, C, and D.
© Douglas Peebles/Corbis

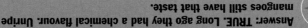

Answer: TRUE. Long ago they had a chemical flavour. Unripe mangoes still have that taste.

21

SEARCH LIGHT

Can you name three citrus fruits?

The Drinkable Fruit

The orange is one of several kinds of small trees and shrubs that belong to the **'citrus'** group. Other common citrus fruits are lemons, limes, grapefruit, and tangerines. The first oranges and other citrus fruits probably grew in the tropical regions of Asia, especially in the islands of Southeast Asia. The practice of growing oranges spread to India, to the east coast of Africa, and then to the Mediterranean regions. Today oranges are also grown in the warm regions of the Americas and Australia.

The orange is a nearly round fruit with a leathery, oily peel and juicy flesh (or pulp) inside. It grows on attractive trees 4.5 to 9 metres tall. Orange trees have sweet-smelling waxy blossoms and leaves that stay green throughout the year. Their branches often have small thorns as well. A single orange tree will bear fruit for 50 to 80 years or longer. Sometimes the age of an orange tree is counted in centuries!

The most popular variety of orange is the China orange. It's also called the sweet orange or common orange. This orange tastes best when it is fully ripe, and it should not be picked before that. Another popular variety, the Seville orange, is not as commonly grown. The Seville is used in making **marmalade**. Other varieties of oranges include the Jaffa from Israel, the blood orange with its red pulp, and the navel, which is usually seedless.

Oranges are also grown to produce juice, either fresh or frozen. Nearly half the oranges produced in the United States are made into frozen **concentrated** juice. Orange juice is rich in vitamin C and also provides some vitamin A.

LEARN MORE! READ THESE ARTICLES...
JACKFRUIT • LEMONS • MANGOES

The seedless navel orange, shown here, became a major fruit in California after it was introduced from Brazil in 1873.
© Ed Young/Corbis

Answer: Oranges, tangerines, lemons, limes, kumquats, and grapefruit are all citrus fruits.

SEARCH LIGHT

Find and correct the error in the following sentence: Runner plants make the strawberry plant hard to catch.

Luscious Fruit Treat

Strawberries are eaten fresh, often with cream. They are also used as a filling for pastries, tarts, and cakes. Strawberry shortcake is made of fresh strawberries, a cake or biscuit base, and whipped cream. Needless to say, strawberries are a very popular fruit.

Strawberry plants can be found throughout most of the United States and Canada, Europe, the United Kingdom, and parts of Africa. They are also grown in New Zealand, Australia, and Japan.

The strawberry is a low **herb** plant that branches off in all directions. At the top of the plant is the 'crown' from which the leaves sprout. The leaves have three sections, each of them hairy with **saw-toothed** edges. The flowers are mostly white and sometimes reddish. They appear in small groups on slender **stalks** arising from the leaves. As the plant gets older, the roots become woody. Then the crown sends out 'runner plants', trailing vines that spread over the ground, making the plant bigger.

Runner plants are planted in autumn for a crop expected the following year. Strawberry plants are usually used to produce fruit for one to four years. In regions with very cold winters, the plants are put out in spring and protected during winter by covering the rows with straw.

Strawberries need to be stored in a cool and dry place after they've been picked. But they still don't remain fresh for very long. Some are frozen or preserved to make them last longer.

LEARN MORE! READ THESE ARTICLES...
APPLES · BANANAS · GRAPES

The heart-shaped red fruits of the strawberry plant are popular all over the world.
© Ed Young/Corbis

Answer: Runner plants make the strawberry plant bigger.

Vegetables or Fruit?

SEARCH LIGHT

The first Europeans to use the tomato as a food were the
a) Spanish and French.
b) Italians and Aztec.
c) Spanish and Italians.
d) Swiss and Indians.

Cooks call the tomato a vegetable, but gardeners say it's a fruit. It's actually both! In the garden the tomato is considered a fruit because it grows from a flower and has seeds in it. But in the kitchen it's considered a vegetable because it isn't sweet like apples or grapes.

Tomatoes were first grown thousands of years ago by South American Indians who lived in the Andes Mountains. In Mexico, Indians **cultivated** tomatoes long before Spanish explorers arrived in the 1500s. The name 'tomato' comes from *tomatl*, a word in the language of the Aztec people of Mexico.

A few tomato varieties.
© Michelle Garrett/Corbis

The Spanish who returned to Europe after their explorations brought the tomato back with them. The tomato was first used as a food in Spain and Italy. From Europe, tomatoes were taken to North America. Today they grow all around the world, wherever winters are not too cold and summers not too hot.

Tomatoes not only taste good - they're also good for you! They're packed with vitamins A and C. Tomatoes can be served cooked by themselves or used as a part of many different meals. They're used to make soups and salads. Tomato juice is popular because of its tangy flavour. Tomatoes also form the base for ketchup, chilli sauce, and spaghetti sauce. And, of course, they're a must for your pizza!

LEARN MORE! READ THESE ARTICLES...
GRAPES • MAIZE • PEPPERS

A father and his son taste a tomato they have just picked. Tomatoes come in many different shapes and sizes.
© Ariel Skelley/Corbis

DID YOU KNOW?
For a long time the tomato was believed to be a relative of the poisonous belladonna plant. In fact, the roots and leaves of the tomato plant are poisonous. But the fruit is safe to eat and, in fact, is very good for you!

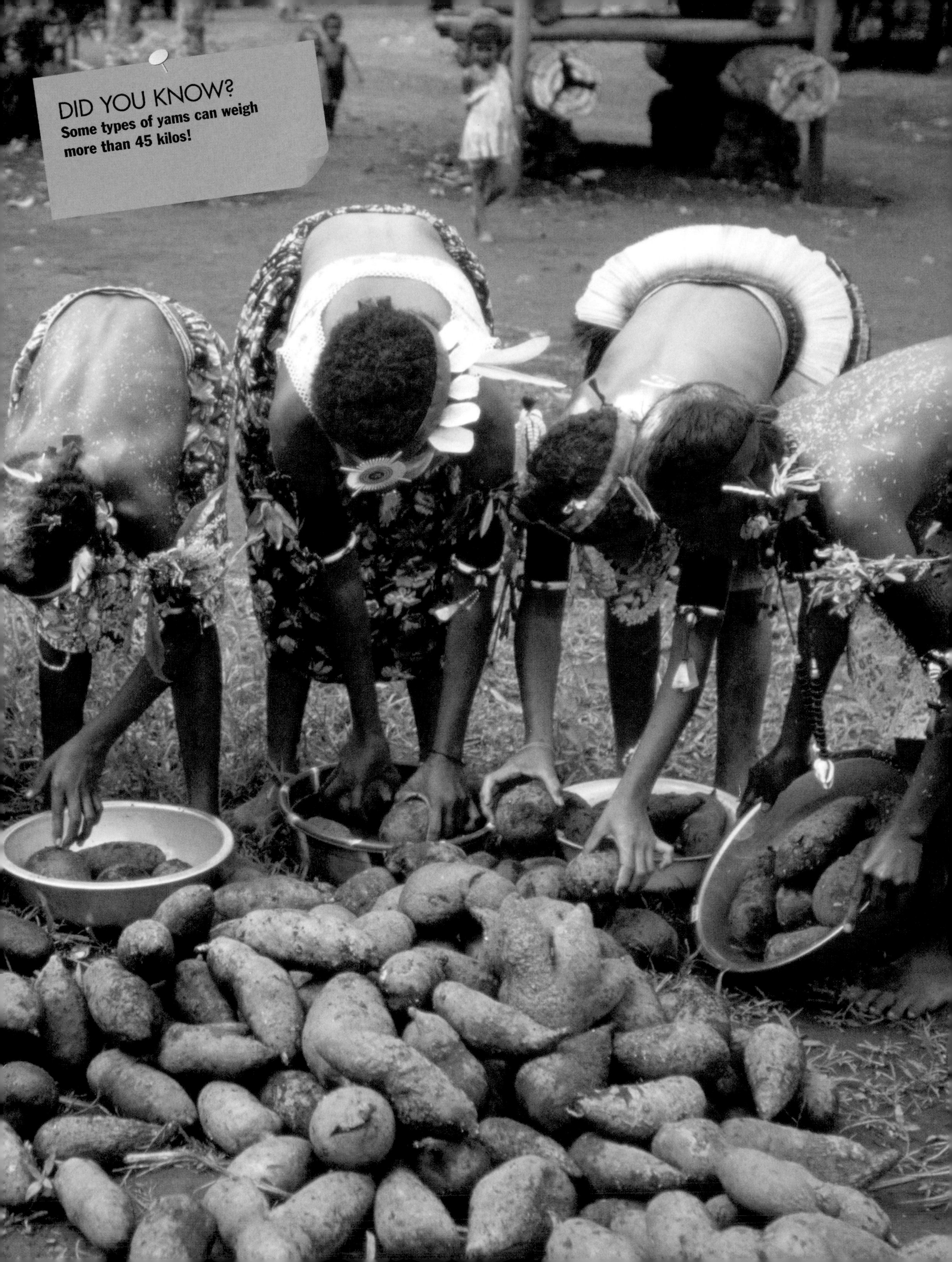

DID YOU KNOW?

Some types of yams can weigh more than 45 kilos!

Tasty Tubers

SEARCH LIGHT

Fill in the gap: The part of a yam that is eaten grows _____.

Yam plants are climbing vines. Long slender stems bear clusters of small green flowers that look quite pretty. The plants need hot wet weather and take rather long to grow. Different varieties of them are grown as food in the tropics.

Baskets of yams at a market in the Cook Islands.
© Robert Holmes/Corbis

In some parts of West Africa and New Guinea, yams are also used in ceremonies related to farming.

Yams, like potatoes, have thick tubers. A tuber is the thick part of the plant's stem that grows underground and stores food for the plant. And just as with the potato, the tuber is the part of a yam that people eat.

There are hundreds of varieties of yam. They differ greatly in look and taste. The colour of the tuber's flesh may be white, yellow, pink, or purple. Some taste sweet, some bitter, and some quite bland.

True yams are different from the sweet potato. However, some varieties of sweet potato are often called yams in the United States. Both sweet potatoes and yams are **starchy** foods with a fair amount of sugar in them. Some yams also contain poisons that may make a person sick if the tuber is not properly cooked. The poisons are destroyed by cooking.

Most people eat yams as they would potatoes. Yams are served fried, roasted, baked, and boiled. Cooked yams are often mashed into a sticky paste or dough that can then be further baked or boiled.

LEARN MORE! READ THESE ARTICLES...
CABBAGE • PEANUTS • PEPPERS

Women collect yams in Papua New Guinea.
© Caroline Penn/Corbis

Answer: The part of a yam that is eaten grows underground.

SEARCH LIGHT

Fill in
the gap:
Barley was
one of the
_____ plants
grown as a crop.

A Versatile Cereal

Barley was one of the first plants ever grown as a crop. Like other food plants in the group called 'cereals', barley is a grass that is grown for its **starchy** seeds. Barley has a nutty taste and a lot of food value. People have known for a long time that barley is good to eat. It was probably first

Barley, one of the world's major cereal plants.
© Doug Wilson/Corbis

grown in **prehistoric** Ethiopia and in Southeast Asia. Egyptian farmers grew barley as far back as 5000 BC. Ancient people of Europe, Asia, and North Africa raised it too.

Barley is an especially widespread crop because it can be grown in so many different climates. It grows and ripens quickly, which makes it just right for areas that have short growing seasons - regions far to the north (such as Canada) or high up in the mountains (such as Tibet). But barley can survive just as well in the dry heat of North Africa.

Ancient people used barley to make bread. Although barley doesn't bake as well as wheat does, the flour is good for making flat breads such as pita. And barley is ideal for making some hot cereals. Polished **kernels** called 'pearl barley' serve to thicken and flavour soups. Barley can also be put through a process that turns it into a flavouring called 'malt'. Barley malt is used in making some vinegars and drinks, especially beer.

Despite all these uses, only about half the barley grown in the world is eaten by people. The rest goes to feed animals.

DID YOU KNOW?
Ancient Roman gladiators trained on a diet of barley. These professional fighters gained energy and strength from barley's excellent food value.

LEARN MORE! READ THESE ARTICLES...
MAIZE • RICE • WHEAT

About half of the world's barley crop is used as animal feed.
© Frank Lane Picture Agency/Corbis

Answer: Barley was one of the first plants grown as a crop.

Grain of the
Americas

Maize is a grain, just as wheat and rice are. Maize is known as 'corn' in the United States, Canada, and Australia. It was first found in the Americas. Mayan farmers of Mexico and Central America **cultivated** maize. Early European explorers of the Americas were the first to take maize to Europe. Since that time, maize has been grown all over the world.

A boy holding ears of corn in a farm field in South Africa.
© Barbara Bannister–Gallo Images/Corbis

Maize grows in areas that have rich soil and cold nights but no frost during the growing season. It also needs plenty of sunshine to ripen. These conditions are found in a large area of the midwestern United States known as the Corn Belt. Similar conditions are also found in parts of Asia, much of Central and South America, the Mediterranean, and southern Africa. The largest producers of maize, after the United States, are China and Brazil.

Maize is used to feed cattle and **poultry**. And, of course, it serves as food for humans. The maize that people eat is also called 'sweet corn'. The grains of maize that people eat are the seeds of the plant. The seeds are called 'kernels' and are found along the length of the spike. The spike with the kernels is commonly known as the 'ear' of corn. Leaves called 'husks' wrap around and cover the spike. The seeds, if they are planted, will grow into new maize plants.

Large quantities of maize are used in Latin American cooking. *Masa harina* is a kind of flour made from maize. It makes a dough that's used to make tortillas - a kind of round thin flat bread. They are the wraps for tacos, burritos, and enchiladas.

LEARN MORE! READ THESE ARTICLES…
BARLEY • RICE • WHEAT

SEARCH LIGHT

Find and correct the error in the following sentence: Maize was first found in Europe.

DID YOU KNOW?
None of the maize plant has to be wasted. For example, the stalks are made into paper and materials for building. And the cobs - the spikes stripped of kernels - are used for fuel and to make charcoal.

Vast fields of maize like this one in the U.S. state of Nebraska are a common sight in the U.S. Corn Belt.
© Philip Gould/Corbis

Answer: Maize was first found in the Americas.

SEARCH LIGHT

When you eat rice, you're eating the seeds of a kind of
a) grass.
b) tea.
c) fruit.

Food from Water-Grown Grasses

Do you chew grass? Actually, you probably do! The grains that most people eat daily are actually grasses - or at least grass seeds. These include wheat, maize, rye, and rice. More than half the people in the world eat rice almost every day. The grain is so important that millions of people in Asia would starve if they didn't have it. China and India are amongst the largest producers of rice. Rice is also the basic feature of most meals in the islands of the western Pacific and much of Latin America.

Rice plants are carried for planting.
© Michael S. Yamashita/Corbis

Most rice is grown in water. The land under the water has to be smooth and level, like a table top. The water on top must be the correct depth. If it's too deep, the rice will drown. If it's not deep enough, the rice won't grow.

In the countries of Asia, the muddy ground is ploughed by water buffalo pulling wooden ploughs. Then the tiny rice plants are planted in rows. If it doesn't rain enough, water is brought in from lakes and rivers to flood the fields. The rice plant grows under the water, with its green shoots sticking out. A water-filled field planted with rice is called a 'rice paddy'.

When the rice is ripe, the water is drained off the fields. After the ground has dried, the rice **stalks** are cut and tied into bundles. When the stalks have dried, the brown **hulls** are removed from the rice seeds. Many farmers grow rice for their families to eat. Rice to be sold in shops goes to a factory. There it is packed into boxes and then shipped to the shops.

DID YOU KNOW?
Rice was first grown as a crop about 5,000 years ago in India. It later spread from there. It reached southern Europe in the 1400s.

LEARN MORE! READ THESE ARTICLES...
BARLEY • MAIZE • WHEAT

In order to grow rice in hilly areas, giant steps called 'terraces' are dug into the hillsides. Each giant step has a little wall of mud at its edge to hold in the water that covers the rice as it is growing.
© Dave G. Houser/Corbis

Answer: a) grass.

Large wheat fields cover parts of Kansas, North Dakota, Montana, Oklahoma, and Washington in the United States.

SEARCH LIGHT

About how many years ago was wheat first grown on farms?
a) 9,000
b) 900
c) 9,000,000

The Bread of Life

Wheat is one of the oldest and most important of the **cereal** crops. Many people eat wheat products at every meal. It is an important ingredient of many breads, pastries, and pastas. Wheat has lots of **nutrients** and is a major source of energy for humans.

Wheat ready for harvesting.
© Bohemian Nomad Picturemakers/Corbis

Wheat can be eaten simply by soaking and cooking the seeds, or grain. But for many foods the grain has to be turned to flour first. This requires grinding the wheat.

The wheat plant is a kind of grass with long slender leaves. In most kinds of wheat the stems are hollow. The top part of the plant is made up of a number of flowers. Two to six flowers form groups called 'spikelets'. Two to three of the flowers in each spikelet produce grains. It's the grains that are used as food.

More of the world's farmland is used for growing wheat than for any other food crop. The world's largest producer of wheat is China. Other leading producers are India, the United States, Russia, France, Ukraine, and Turkey.

Many thousands of varieties of wheat are known. The most important ones are used to make bread and pasta. Club wheat, a soft variety, is used for cakes, biscuits, pastries, and household flour.

Wheat was first grown on farms about 9,000 years ago in the Euphrates River valley of the Middle East. In ancient Egypt, wheat was so important that the people buried some with the pharaohs (kings). In this way, they believed, the pharaohs would never go hungry in the afterlife.

DID YOU KNOW?
Although most wheat is eaten, some of it is used to make paste. (Be careful not to confuse the two!)

LEARN MORE! READ THESE ARTICLES...
BARLEY • MAIZE • RICE

DID YOU KNOW?
For hundreds of years, chocolate was enjoyed mainly as a beverage. By the 1500s the Aztec of Mexico were making a bitter cocoa-bean drink. They also used cocoa beans as money.

The Chocolate Tree

A chocolate tree may sound like something made up in a book or film, but chocolate really does come from trees. A tree called the 'cacao' is the source of all cocoa powder and chocolate.

Cacao trees grow only in warm areas that get a lot of rain. The trees grow long fruit called 'pods' that range in colour from bright yellow to deep purple. Inside the pods are rows of seeds called 'cocoa beans'. Each is about the size and shape of a big fingernail. It is from these cocoa beans that we get one of the world's favourite foods, chocolate.

But a lot of things have to be done to the beans before they turn into chocolate. After the cocoa beans are taken out of the pods, they are left in a damp place for a few days. The beans turn a rich brown colour and begin to smell like chocolate. Then they are dried and cleaned.

Next the beans are shipped to chocolate factories all over the world. There they are roasted and ground into a paste. This paste contains a fatty yellow liquid called 'cocoa butter'. To make chocolate, you have to add extra cocoa butter to the paste. To make dry cocoa powder, you have to remove all the cocoa butter.

The chocolate is still not ready to eat, though. Cocoa beans are not naturally sweet. In fact, the paste is very bitter. So a lot of sugar must be mixed in. Milk may be added too. The chocolate is then poured into moulds to harden into chocolate bars. Now it is finally ready to eat!

LEARN MORE! READ THESE ARTICLES…
COFFEE • NUTS • TEA

SEARCH LIGHT

True or false? Chocolate is naturally very sweet.

Answer: FALSE. Chocolate is naturally quite bitter. It is the sugar added to it that makes it sweet.

DID YOU KNOW?
The saguaro cactus blossom is the state flower of Arizona, U.S., where it is illegal to kill the saguaro cactus.

Don't Touch!

Cactus plants nearly always grow in dry areas where it hardly ever rains. In all there are about 1,650 different kinds of cactus plants (cacti). All of them except one live in North and South America, especially in Mexico. Cacti can be very tall or really tiny. Some have strange shapes or features. In the Arizona desert of the United States, you can see miles of giant treelike saguaro cacti. Another type, the old-man cactus, got its name from its woolly white 'hair'. Some prickly pear cacti have a fruit that can be eaten. You can even make sugary sweets from a cactus.

Most plants give off water through their leaves. But water is rare and **precious** in the deserts where cacti live. Cacti save water by having no leaves or only small ones that drop off early. A cactus also stores up water inside its thick stem. Almost every cactus has sharp spines that look like thorns or needles. These help protect it from people and animals that want to eat the moist parts inside. In the old days in the American West, the watery juice inside a barrel cactus often saved people's lives.

Some types of cacti are used for making medicines. Dried-up cacti are sometimes used as firewood, and cacti planted around houses can provide a thorny fence. Many people like to keep cacti as houseplants for their unusual appearance. Some cacti also produce big colourful flowers. Maybe you could grow a cactus garden!

LEARN MORE! READ THESE ARTICLES…
JACKFRUIT • PEPPERS • SUGARCANE

SEARCH LIGHT

There are more than how many different kinds of cacti in the world?
a) 650
b) 16,500
c) 1,650

Which part of the coffee plant is used to make the coffee drink?

More than 10 billion coffee trees are grown on plantations all over the world. Each tree yields about 450 grams of coffee every year. Trees begin to bear fruit when 3 to 5 years old and continue to do so for another 10 to 15 years. Here, a woman in Thailand handpicks coffee cherries, which contain coffee beans.
© Michael S. Yamashita/Corbis

The World's Favourite Cup

Coffee is one of the most popular drinks in the world. Many people think it has a great taste and a wonderful smell. Coffee also contains caffeine, which is a stimulant - that is, a substance that increases the body's activity.

Coffee grows as a bush with sweet-smelling flowers and fleshy fruit called 'coffee cherries'. Within the fruit are two seeds, or 'beans'. The

Coffee beans ready for purchase.
© Mark Forri/Corbis

beans are dried, roasted, and ground. The ground coffee is then **brewed** in water to make a drink. Coffee plants need warm weather and plenty of rain, so they grow only in **tropical** regions. There are at least 60 types of coffee plants. But only two kinds, called Arabica and Robusta, are in great demand.

Arabica coffee has more flavour and **fragrance**. It is grown in Central and South America, the Caribbean, and Indonesia. Coffee from Colombia is especially well known. Robusta coffee is grown mainly in Africa. The Robusta plant does not pick up disease easily. It is also useful in making instant coffee. Instant coffee is coffee powder that dissolves completely in water.

Coffee probably first came from Ethiopia, in north-eastern Africa. From there it was taken to the Middle East. At first it was used as a food, as a medicine, and in wines. People did not begin to drink coffee as we know it for hundreds of years. Coffee was taken to Europe and then the Americas starting in about the 1500s.

Today coffee is one of the world's most popular drinks. Rest periods taken during working hours are often called 'coffee breaks'. Many, many people begin each day by drinking a cup of coffee.

DID YOU KNOW?
Many countries have special coffee drinks. Turkish coffee is a strong, thick sweetened drink. Italy's espresso is made by forcing steam through ground coffee beans. France's *café au lait* and Latin America's *café con leche* both mean 'coffee with milk'.

LEARN MORE! READ THESE ARTICLES...
CACAO • SUGARCANE • TEA

Answer: The coffee seeds, or beans, are used to make coffee.

Spectacular Leaves, Sensational Syrup

In parts of the United States and Canada autumn is spectacular as the leaves on the trees turn bright yellow, red, and orange. One tree in particular displays fantastic autumn colours - the maple. Some maple trees even display unusual colours such as burgundy, bronze, and purple.

There are about 200 kinds of maple tree. They can be found throughout most of North America, Europe, and north-eastern Asia. The leaves of most maples grow thickly in a **dome** shape. In summer the thick **foliage** of the maple provides lots of shade. This makes it a popular tree for parks and streets. Many people also plant maple trees in their gardens.

The fruit of maple trees is a hard pebble-sized structure with a pair of thin wings. Each wing has a seed at its tip. The wings help the seeds 'fly' away on the wind, far enough from the tree to grow in the sunlight.

Many maples produce sweet **sap**. In North America the sap of the sugar maple is made into maple syrup. Sugar maples grow slowly. They do not produce sap until they are about 40 years old!

North American Indians long ago learned the secret of tapping maple trees for their sugar. The process is fairly simple. Several holes are drilled into the bark of the tree. **Spouts** are driven into these holes, and the sap flows through the spouts into pails hanging on the spouts. The sap is boiled until it has thickened. Then the maple syrup is ready to pour onto your pancakes!

LEARN MORE! READ THESE ARTICLES...
APPLES • CACAO • SUGARCANE

SEARCH LIGHT

Why
are the seeds
of a maple tree
attached to wings?

Answer: The wings help the seeds 'fly' on the wind so they can travel to a sunnier place, where they can grow.

The Original Fast Food

Before people learned to hunt or fish, they lived mostly on fruits, nuts, and berries. Nuts were especially important because they are very nourishing and rich in oil and protein. Nuts also keep well and are easy to store. A nut is actually a kind of fruit. It is dry and hard, and it is usually covered with a tough woody shell.

DID YOU KNOW?
The kola nut, grown widely in the tropics, has been used to flavour fizzy drinks. But many of these drinks now contain chemicals that taste like the kola nut instead.

A couple of nuts that you may know about are chestnuts and pistachios. There are several kinds of chestnut tree, including the American, European, Chinese, and Japanese varieties. Chestnuts are an important food for people and animals. The American and European chestnuts provide valuable wood. And some chestnut trees are grown simply for their beauty.

Pistachio trees are from Central Asia, where they have been grown for about 3,000 years. Today they are also grown in North America. Their nuts are greenish and very tasty.

Other kinds of nuts include hazelnuts, beechnuts, and acorns. But some foods that are popularly called 'nuts' aren't true nuts. Peanuts, for example, are actually a type of bean! And coconuts are really a kind of stone fruit called a 'drupe'. The Brazil nut is also called the candlenut because it can be lit and used as a candle. But it's technically a seed.

Walnuts are another 'nut' that's not really a nut. But they too are good food. They have been grown since ancient times. They were highly valued in Persia and Mesopotamia. Today they are grown in many countries. Black walnut trees are also planted as decorations, and their fruit **husks** are used for making dyes. The trees grow slowly and may live for more than 250 years!

True or false? Peanuts are tasty and nutritious nuts.

LEARN MORE! READ THESE ARTICLES...
OLIVE · PALM · PEANUTS

Some foods that are called 'nuts' are actually other kinds of foods. These include walnuts and coconuts.
EB Inc.

Answer: FALSE. The peanut is not really a nut – it's a kind of bean.

Groves of olive trees cover the hills near the city of Jaén in southern Spain.

SEARCH LIGHT

True or false? People eat olives right off the tree.

Plant of Peace and Plenty

Since ancient times people have grown olive trees for their fruit and oil. Today olive trees are found in all the countries bordering the Mediterranean Sea. The trees are also grown in parts of the United States, Australia, and South Africa. But the leading producers of olives and olive oil are Spain, Italy, and Greece. They sell a lot of the fruit and oil to other countries.

Olive branches ripe with fruit.
© Vittoriano Rastelli/Corbis

The common olive tree has broad leaves and many branches. Its leaves are dark green above and silvery underneath. Olive branches have been a **universal** symbol of peace since the days of ancient Greece.

Olive trees bloom in late spring. The tiny white flowers hang in clusters and develop into fruit that is either picked by hand or shaken from the tree. An olive tree does not always bear fruit every year. The trees may produce a heavy crop one year and no crop the next year.

Often the olives are picked when they are still unripe and green coloured. Some crops are allowed to ripen and darken on the trees before they're picked. But fresh olives are very bitter. Before they can be eaten, they must be treated with chemicals and stored, sometimes for several months. By the time they're ready to eat, their colour may be green, black, dark red, or even purplish.

Olives are grown for the production of olive oil as well. The oil is taken from the fruit. It is one of the most widely used oils for cooking and eating, especially by people in the Mediterranean region. In using this oil, they are carrying on a tradition that is as old as civilization.

LEARN MORE! READ THESE ARTICLES...
LEMONS • NUTS • PALM

DID YOU KNOW?

The olive tree is an evergreen and keeps its leaves all year-round. It can grow to be 15 metres tall and may live more than 500 years!

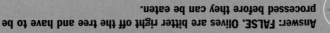

Answer: FALSE. Olives are bitter right off the tree and have to be processed before they can be eaten.

SEARCH LIGHT

Fill in the gap: The _____ is one of the most valuable palms in the world.

The leaves of palms are usually clustered at the top of the tree's trunk in a large fan- or feather-shaped crown. The palm trees shown here are growing on a beach in St. Croix.

The Prince of Plants

The palm is one of the most useful plants around, which is why people sometimes call it the 'prince of the plant kingdom'. There are many types of palm. They grow as trees, shrubs, and vines in the tropics and other warm regions.

The trunk of the palm is branchless, with a **tuft** of large leaves on the top. The trunks can be very tall, or they can be so short that the plant is almost trunkless. Often the palm trunk is smooth. But the trunks of some are spiny like a cactus while others are covered with stiff **fibres** that can be

Palm trees grow from sand on a beach in Jamaica.
© Eye Ubiquitous/Corbis

made into strong cords. Palm leaves are **pleated** and may be shaped like fans or feathers. Some varieties of palm leaves are very long with prickly tips.

Palms produce dry or fleshy fruits that vary in size, shape, and structure. For example, the date and the betel nut are soft fleshy fruits. The fruit of the coconut is hard on the outside and has moist 'meat' and liquid inside. The coco-de-mer is the largest fruit in the world. This palm fruit can be larger than a human head, with a pair of seeds that look like two coconuts joined together.

The coconut is one of the most valuable palms in the world. It provides vegetable oil for cooking. The fibre of the coconut husk is called 'coir' and can be woven into ropes and mats. The coconut shell is hard and is used to make cups and bottles. The liquid in the centre is called 'coconut milk'. You can drink it and cook with it, much as you would with animal milk.

LEARN MORE! READ THESE ARTICLES…
BANANAS • NUTS • OLIVE

DID YOU KNOW?
Some island people say there are as many uses for coconuts as there are days in a year.

Answer: The coconut is one of the most valuable palms in the world.

When Is a Nut Not a Nut?

SEARCH LIGHT

Find and correct the errors in the following sentence: Peanuts are legumes that grow on trees in cold sandy places.

They look and taste like nuts. They have shells like nuts, and they have skins like nuts. But they're not nuts. They're *peanuts*.

Actual nuts grow mostly on trees or bushes. But peanuts grow underground. That's why peanuts are also called 'groundnuts'. Although they look and taste like nuts, peanuts are really part of a plant group called 'legumes'. Legumes also include peas and beans. The peanut pod is a spongy shell covered with tiny dimples. Inside the shell you will usually find two peanuts. These are the seeds for new peanut plants.

A woman harvests peanuts on the island of Mauritius.
© Wolfgang Kaehler/Corbis

Peanuts grow easily in warm sandy places. They require at least five months of warm weather, with rainfall during the growing season. The peanut plant is a low bush. Some kinds grow long low branches called 'runners'. When the peanuts are ripe, peanut farmers usually dig up the plants and stack them against sticks to dry out. Farmers feed the tops of the dry plants to their animals.

Peanuts may be roasted in their shells before they're eaten. Or they may be shelled and prepared as salted peanuts. Roasted peanuts are used in sweets and baked goods, for peanut butter, and in many other foods. Peanuts are often grown just for their oil.

An important person in the history of the peanut is Dr. George Washington Carver. This American researcher suggested that farmers plant peanuts to help make their worn-out soil healthy again. And then he came up with new uses for peanuts so that the farmers could sell them. By the time he'd finished, Dr. Carver had found more than 300 things that could be made out of peanuts.

LEARN MORE! READ THESE ARTICLES...
NUTS • TOMATOES • YAMS

Peanuts are grown in warm temperate or subtropical areas throughout the world. Here workers pick weeds in a peanut field in Samoa.
© Catherine Karnow/Corbis

DID YOU KNOW?
Dr. George Washington Carver's products from peanuts included peanut milk, cheese, and coffee, as well as plastics, shampoo, and shoe polish.

Answer: Peanuts are legumes that grow underground in warm sandy places.

Hot and Spicy

Garden peppers have been used in cooking since ancient times. Hot peppers contain a substance called 'capsaicin' that gives them a sharp burning taste. Many people enjoy this strong taste and use it to flavour foods. People like to eat peppers fresh, dried, smoked, tinned, powdered, and pickled.

Pepper plants are herbs. The fruit of the plants differs in size, shape, and taste. The colour ranges from green through yellow to deep red and

There are two general types of peppers: the mild and the hot varieties.
© Paul Almasy/Corbis

purple. You'll find peppers in the tropics of Asia. They also grow all over Central and South America. In 1493 pepper seeds were carried from South America to Spain. After that, the plants quickly spread all over Europe.

There are two kinds of pepper: mild and hot. Mild peppers are usually large and can be red, green, or yellow in colour. Bell peppers are bell-shaped, wrinkled, and puffy. Pimiento is a mild pepper with a special flavour and is usually used for stuffing other foods, such as olives. Paprika is another mild pepper. It's usually powdered and used as a spice. It is especially popular in Spain and Hungary.

The hot peppers include cherry, red cluster, tabasco, long chilli, and cayenne peppers. These are often served as relishes and pickles or ground into a fine powdered spice. Tabasco peppers are ground and mixed with vinegar to make a spicy hot sauce. Both fresh and dried Mexican chilli peppers are used to flavour stewed meat dishes.

LEARN MORE! READ THESE ARTICLES...
MAIZE • RICE • TOMATOES

SEARCH LIGHT

Fill in the gap: _____ is what makes hot peppers hot.

Bell peppers like the ones shown are often used in salads, as cases for fillings, and in other cooked dishes.
© Michelle Garrett/Corbis

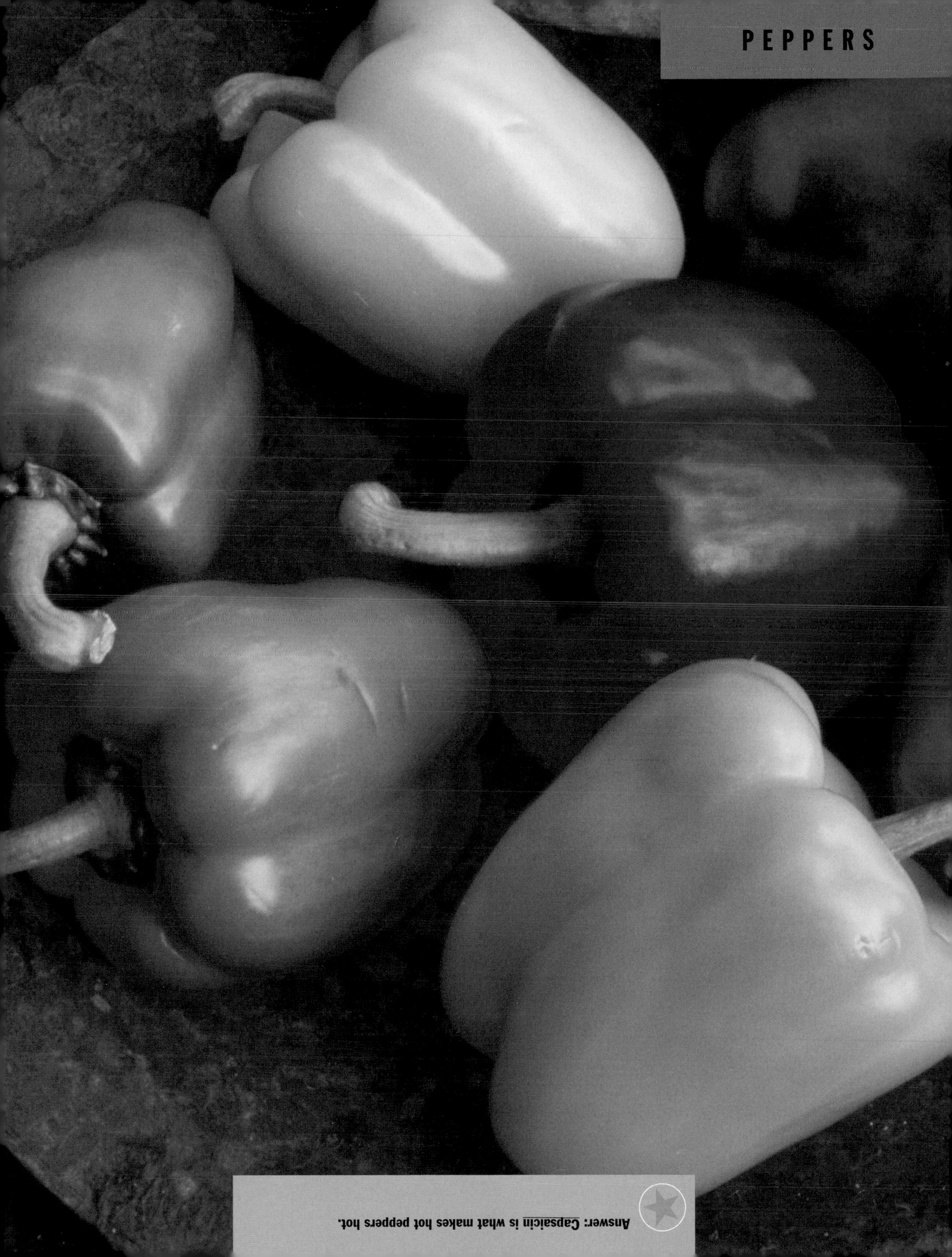

Answer: Capsaicin is what makes hot peppers hot.

SEARCH LIGHT

There are many different kinds of seaweed. Can you name three of them?

Wild Plants of the Ocean

You are in the waves at the seaside when suddenly something that feels cold and clammy slaps you on the back! Is it a friendly fish? No, it's probably just seaweed. These plants grow wild in the sea, just as weeds grow wild on land.

Seaweed on a New Zealand beach.
© Richard Hamilton Smith/Corbis

Seaweed grows all over the world. Some kinds float along the top of the water. Others are attached to the sea bottom or to rocks. Seaweed comes in many colours, such as red, brown, purple, and green. It may look like a red carpet or like tree branches with leaves and berries. The 'berries' are actually little gas-filled balloons that help keep the leaves afloat. Some kinds of seaweed, called 'kelp', can grow longer than 30 metres and have tough and leathery branches. Other kinds look like lettuce and are actually called 'sea lettuce'.

People have found many uses for seaweed. The plants have been used for stuffing furniture and making paper. Giant kelps have been used as ropes. Laver, dulse, gulfweed, sea lettuce, and other kinds of seaweed are eaten, either by themselves or as part of other foods. Brown seaweed is used for making **fertilizers** for plants.

Even animals take advantage of seaweed. Tangled clumps of seaweed provide homes and hiding places for fish and other sea creatures. In the Atlantic Ocean, a huge floating mass of gulfweed between the United States and Africa is a resting place for seabirds. This gulfweed is called *Sargassum*, and this part of the Atlantic is the famous Sargasso Sea.

DID YOU KNOW?
If you like sushi or maki rolls, then you've probably eaten seaweed. Many of these Japanese delicacies are wrapped in seaweed.

LEARN MORE! READ THESE ARTICLES...
CACTUS • PALM • RICE

Giant kelp grows off the coast of California.
© Ralph A. Clevenger/Corbis

Answer: Kelp, sea lettuce, laver, dulse, and gulfweed are all names for different kinds of seaweed.

A Sweet and Syrupy Plant

The sugarcane plant is a giant grass that grows year-round in warm and wet regions of the world. The island of New Guinea is probably the original home of sugarcane. Gradually, the plant was introduced to Southeast Asia, India, Polynesia, and other areas. Today Asia is the largest producer of sugarcane, followed by South and North America.

Workers harvesting sugarcane.
© Otto Lang/Corbis

The sugarcane plant is grown for its sweet **sap**. Much of the world's sugar and molasses comes from sugarcane sap. And in many parts of the world, people enjoy sucking on a piece of sugarcane for a sweet treat.

Sugarcane grows in clumps of stalks that reach a height of 3 to 6 metres. The colour of the stalk varies from almost white to yellow to deep green, purple, red, or violet.

The sugarcane crop needs at least 150 centimetres of water per year and nine months for the stalks to ripen. Once the stalks are ripe, they are stripped of their leaves and trimmed. The stalks are then washed and cut into short lengths. Most of this work is still done by hand.

Sugar is removed from the cane by two methods. In the first method, the finely cut stalks are put in hot water. This separates the sugar from the stalks. In the second method, the juice is squeezed from the stalks by pressing them between heavy rollers.

The juice taken from the cane is heated until it is boiling. Next, the water in the juice is allowed to **evaporate**. The resulting syrup is boiled again until sugar crystals have formed. The syrup left behind is called 'molasses'.

DID YOU KNOW?

Raw sugar is brown, not white.

LEARN MORE! READ THESE ARTICLES...
CACAO • MAPLE • STRAWBERRIES

Sugarcane is sold at market in a village in India.
© Earl & Nazima Kowall/Corbis

SEARCH LIGHT

Fill in
the gaps:
We get
_____ and
_____ from
sugarcane sap.

Answer: We get sugar and molasses from sugarcane sap.

SEARCH LIGHT

What's
the difference
between
green tea
and black tea?

The Cup That Cheers

It soothes you when you are upset. And if you're tired, it can lift your spirits. It's tea - the drink that cheers!

Tea was first drunk in China thousands of years ago. At first it was used as a **medicinal** drink, but eventually it became popular to drink anytime. It was later introduced to Japan. European trading ships took it from Asia to England and Holland.

Worker separating tea leaves by hand in Indonesia.
© Owen Franken/Corbis

There are two main varieties of tea - the small-leaved China plant and the large-leaved Assam plant. Mixing the leaves of these produces many other types of tea.

Tea can be named according to where it's grown. For example, there's China tea, Ceylon tea, Japanese tea, Indonesian tea, and African tea. But most tea is known as green, black, or oolong tea. Green tea, made from the China plant, is produced in Japan, China, Malaysia, and Indonesia. Black tea, made from the Assam plant, comes mostly from India. Oolong teas are produced mostly in southern China and Taiwan.

The different kinds of tea are made in different ways. To make black tea, the freshly picked leaves are dried, rolled, and strained. They are then fermented. Fermenting is a way of making the flavour more intense. Finally, the leaves are dried with hot air. This is how the tea becomes black. Unlike black tea, green tea is not fermented. The leaves are just rolled and dried, so they remain green. Oolong is made like black tea. It is sometimes scented with flowers such as jasmine.

Tea is made ready for drinking by soaking its leaves in boiled water. This is called 'steeping'.

LEARN MORE! READ THESE ARTICLES...
CACAO • COFFEE • SUGARCANE

DID YOU KNOW?
Iced tea was made popular by an Englishman at the St. Louis World's Fair of 1904 in the United States. His job was to get people to drink tea. The weather was hot, so he filled tall glasses with ice and poured hot tea over it. Everyone loved it!

Tea is made from the young leaves and leaf buds of tea plants. The farmworkers shown here are harvesting tea leaves in Malaysia.
© Neil Rabinowitz/Corbis

Answer: Aside from their different colours, black tea is fermented and green tea is not.

G L O S S A R Y

brew to prepare by steeping (soaking) or boiling in hot water

calorie unit used to measure the amount of heat energy that food provides to the body

carbohydrates plentiful, energy-producing natural substances that are formed by many food plants eaten by animals

cereal starchy seeds of certain grass plants grown for food

citrus kind of tree or shrub grown in warm regions and having thick rind (skin) and fleshy fruits, including oranges, grapefruits, and lemons

climate average weather in a particular area

concentrated condensed, or made thicker, by removal of water

cultivate in gardening and farming, to plant crops and to care for them as they grow

cutting in gardening and farming, a section of an adult plant capable of developing into a new individual

dome large rounded structure shaped like half of a ball

evaporate change into a vapour, or gaseous form, usually by means of heating

fertilizer natural or artificial substance used to make soil better for growing crops

fibre strand or thread-like structure

fodder coarse food for farm animals

foliage the leaves of a plant

fragrance (adjective: fragrant) sweet, pleasant, and often flowery or fruity smell

hemisphere half of the planet Earth or of any other globe-shaped object

herb pleasant-smelling plant (such as mint, oregano, basil, and coriander) often used in cooking, either in part or as a whole

hull hard outer shell of a seed; also, the outer layer of a boat or ship

husk usually thin, dry outer covering of a fruit or seed

kernel whole grain or seed of a cereal plant

marmalade clear, usually sugary jelly containing pieces of fruit and fruit rind

medicinal used as a medicine

nursery place where plants are grown for farming, for scientific experiments, or for sale to the public

nutrient substance that a living thing needs in order to stay healthy and grow

plantation large farming property, usually worked by resident labourers

pleated folded and laid over another part of some material, especially a piece of cloth

poultry birds reared for their eggs or meat

precious of great value or high price

prehistoric having to do with times before written history

pulp 1) in plants, the juicy fleshy part of a soft fruit; 2) in industry, a mashed-up pasty glop such as the plant material used in making paper

rind the usually hard or tough outer layer or "skin" of a fruit or vegetable

sap the liquid inside a plant

saw-toothed having an edge or outline like the teeth (cutting points) of a saw

spout tube, pipe, or hole through which liquid flows

stalk plant's main stem

starchy containing starch, a natural substance that is made by green plants and is part of many foods

Stone Age the oldest period in which human beings are known to have existed, characterized by the making of stone tools

tropical having to do with the Earth's warmest and most humid (moist) climates

tuft 1) in plants, a small cluster of flexible leaves or fibres that are attached or close together at the base and free at the opposite end; 2) in animals, a short mound of fur

universal present or occurring everywhere

INDEX